# Create Your Own

**(A step-by-step guide to using the Law of Attraction
to manifest the things you want)**

**By Eliza-Jane Jackson**

# Preface:

Bad habits are hard to break (and negative thinking is definitely a bad habit!) but break these bad habits, we can. Are you tired of the unhappiness that cynicism creates? I was so I started experimenting with all kinds of spiritual and success principles. This eventually led me to creating Prosperity Wheels. I concluded that the worst thing that was going to happen was I would end up feeling stupid. So, nothing ventured nothing gained, and what a journey it's been!

Picturing or visualising your own prosperity is a powerful way to bring it to you. One very good way to do this is to create a Prosperity Wheel. This visual image of what you want acts as a constant reminder to the Universe. It also encourages you to focus on abundance and happiness instead of lack and misery.

So, what is a Prosperity Wheel? A Prosperity Wheel is a poster board on which you paste a collage of images that you've taken from magazines and other sources. This collage represents the things that you would like to have in your life. This may be good health, a sense of wellbeing, financial wealth or material goods.

John Assaraf brought the age-old concept of a Vision Board (Prosperity Wheel) into the public eye by telling his story in 'The Secret'. If you don't already know John's story you will find a précis of it in chapter 8.

The purpose of writing 'Create Your Own Prosperity Wheel' is to provide you with an easy to follow step-by-step guide to creating your own Prosperity Wheels (Vision Boards). Prosperity Wheels are easy, inexpensive and fun to make but their potential value is immeasurable.

The process of creating a Prosperity Wheel can be done as exercise on your own or with a group of friends; each creating their own wheel. You could even do this as a goal setting exercise with a group of colleagues. All you need to do in this case is select pictures relevant to your work goals (or your organisation's business goals).

## Publisher's Note:

Please note that much of this publication is based on the author's personal experiences and anecdotal evidence. The views expressed in this book are those of the author.

The author has made every reasonable attempt to achieve complete accuracy of the content in this Guide prior to going to press. The publisher and the author cannot accept responsibility for any errors or omissions, however caused.

Also, you should use this information as you see fit, and at your own risk. Your particular situation may not be exactly the same as the examples illustrated here; in fact, it's likely that they won't be the same. Therefore, you should adjust your use of this information and recommendations accordingly.

Finally, use your own wisdom as guidance. Nothing in this Guide is intended to replace common sense, legal, medical or other professional advice. This Guide is meant to inform and entertain the reader.

No responsibility for loss or damage occasioned to any person acting, or refraining from action, as a result of the material in this publication can be accepted by the publisher, the author or the editor.

## Dedication:

This book is dedicated to Rosemary Jackson and Dennis Shepherd.

To mum, thank you for your unstinting support and belief in me, even when I didn't believe in myself! To Dennis, thank you for your support and practical help in getting this project off the ground.

Love to you both.

To everyone who has contributed to this book in some way, many thanks. I hope you're manifesting all the things you want!

E-J

# About the Author:

Eliza-Jane has been a spiritual explorer for most of her life. From an early age she has been interested in trying to influence the direction of her life (although not initially aware that it had a name - the Law of Attraction).

Growing up in a household where one parent had no religious or spiritual beliefs and the other parent had deep spiritual beliefs provided an interesting and thought provoking environment for a curious mind.

As a young girl Eliza-Jane was bullied at school; although her parents were unaware of this. She started asking the Universe to ensure that her tormentors never had access to her outside the classroom. For unrelated reasons, a few months later her parents announced that she was changing schools. End of problem!

Like millions of other people, Eliza-Jane saw The Secret documentary and read the book. Even before that she was captivated by the idea of 'attracting success' through the power of the mind. At first Eliza-Jane used to write affirmations and requests on scraps of paper.

Extensive research on the subject of the 'Law of Attraction' and 'Cosmic Ordering' prompted her to take a more structured approach to her requests to the Universe. At this point she started creating her own Prosperity Wheels (Visions Boards) and she's never looked back since.

Eliza-Jane has been creating personal Prosperity Wheels for many years and has gained a great deal from the experience, as well as having lots of fun creating them.

"I don't claim to be a 'guru' but, based on my own experiences, I really feel that I have something valuable to share with you... that will help you to enjoy more of the life you want. I hope you have as much fun selecting your pictures and assembling your wheel as I have. Thank you for reading my book" (Eliza-Jane Jackson).

# Table of Contents

# 1. Introduction

Before we get into what a Prosperity Wheel is, I will deal with 'prosperity'. I know some people assume prosperity means wealth and greed, and so feel uncomfortable with the idea of prosperity.

Prosperity doesn't necessarily mean financial wealth. Prosperity is defined as any kind of success, good fortune or wealth. Money is only a part of what it means to be prosperous. Prosperity includes your state of mind, your health and your financial situation.

Thoughts become things! Your personal successes, emotional wellbeing or financial prosperity are all the result of your true beliefs. Equally, any lack of these things is also due to your thoughts. This is known as the Law of Attraction.

I believe prosperity and abundance is something we all want in our lives, no matter where we live or who we are. Of course, prosperity and abundance means something different to each of us.

Through the power of your mind you create and shape your life, with every thought every minute of every day. You may not even be conscious of what you're manifesting, and I'm sure sometimes you don't like what you get.

Wouldn't it be nice to use conscious creative visualisation to manifest the successes you want! Well, the good news is you can but first you must believe that you can achieve your goals and aspirations.

So, what exactly is the Law of Attraction? The Law of Attraction states that we attract into our lives anything that we give sufficient attention to; regardless of whether it's positive or negative. Much has already been written on the subject of the Law of Attraction and prosperity. In the Further Reading chapter of this book I have recommended other authors and websites that you might be interested in.

Used in the right way, the Law of Attraction can improve your life. It can be used to attract the success and prosperity you desire.

Creative visualisation has the power to alter your home or work environment, and your circumstances.

Creative visualisation can cause events to happen and attract love into your life. It can also be used to attract money, possessions, work and people into your life. Your options are only limited by your own imagination.

Picturing or visualising your own prosperity is a powerful way to bring it to you. One of the best ways to do this is to create a Prosperity Wheel, but what is it and how does it work? Simply put, a Prosperity Wheel is a creative visualisation tool to help you manifest the things you want.

A Prosperity Wheel is a poster board on which you paste a collage of images that you've taken from magazines and other sources. This collage represents the things that you would like to have in your life. This may be good health, a sense of wellbeing, financial wealth or material goods.

The purpose of your Prosperity Wheel is to activate the Law of Attraction. By selecting pictures and words or phrases that charge your emotions you will begin to manifest (attract) these things into your life. Your intention really is that powerful.

The images can be very specific – as in my example below. They can also be images that evoke a feeling – like a picture of a person meditating that makes you feel deeply peaceful.

This visual image of what you want acts as a constant reminder to the Universe. It also encourages you to focus on abundance and happiness instead of lack and misery. Both of these strengthen the intent.

When you think about it, most people never pause long enough to ask themselves what they want as they're too busy just getting on with things. I think this is because most people don't believe they really can create their own happiness, wealth, or anything else for that matter.

I'm naturally optimistic, but I wanted to try to manifest some of the things that were important to me rather than leaving everything to chance. In my experience Prosperity Wheels move you out of the 'c'est la vie' (such is life) into the 'look what I've manifested/created'.

The idea is that when you surround yourself with images your life changes to match these images and desires. This can apply to anything in your life, including what you want, where you want to live, or where you want to holiday. For many years I wanted to live in Stratford-upon-Avon (Shakespeare Country). Eventually I put this on my Prosperity Wheel and within six months I moved to where I wanted to be.

A success that really stands out for me was the Prosperity Wheel I created when I was struggling to sell my house. Maybe it wasn't the decision to change Estate Agent for the third and final time. Maybe it wasn't the scissors, glue or the magazines. Maybe wasn't the daily reminder of the image of my house with a 'Sold' notice plastered across it that attracted the buyer. Then again…maybe it was. I, for one, choose to believe it was.

You don't need any previous experience or skills to create a Prosperity Wheel. However, it definitely helps if you approach the process with an open mind.

Prosperity Wheels are cheap to make but their potential value to you is immeasurable. Most importantly, making a Prosperity Wheel is fun! It's an exercise that you can do alone or with a group of friends or colleagues. Both will be equally successful as long as you're sufficiently committed to the images you choose.

Figure out what you want in your life and then commit yourself 100% to activating the Law of Attraction. Next, create your Prosperity Wheel and start to manifest your dreams into reality. The possibilities really are endless.

You can create as many Prosperity Wheels as you like. Some people like a different Prosperity Wheel for each aspect of their life. Others prefer to a single collage that captures all their aspirations; the choice is yours.

You can take your Prosperity Wheel down at any time and simply create a new one to meet your changing requirements. Alternatively, you can keep your old Prosperity Wheels forever like John Assaraf (one of the teachers in The Secret).

A few words of caution: you need to be very clear that a Prosperity Wheel is a very powerful thing. It needs to be made and used with respect. It is vital that you ask for things for the highest good. Otherwise you're practising magic rather than spirituality and the consequences for you and others could be unpleasant.

Negative feelings, self-doubt, and criticism can damage the delicate energy that your Prosperity Wheel emits. If you fear scorn, criticism or justification of your Prosperity Wheel from other people then put it somewhere only you can see it. Having tried it, you may decide Prosperity Wheels aren't for you, but please don't allow others to put you off having a go.

Finally, not everyone refers to these collages as Prosperity Wheels. You may also hear them referred to as Vision Boards, Treasure Maps, Dream Boards, Magic Wheels, a Wheel of Fortune, a Visual Explorer, an Image Bank or a Creativity Collage. There are probably many more names that I'm not yet aware of. Whatever the name, they all amount to the same thing – a way of telling the Universe what's truly important to you right now.

Good luck creating your own prosperity!

"The primary cause of unhappiness is never the situation but your thoughts about it." - Eckhart Tolle (German/Canadian author of The Power of Now and A New Earth).

# 2. Prosperity Wheels

## 2.1 Types of Prosperity Wheel

A Prosperity Wheel is a creative visualisation tool to help you manifest the things you want. How you create your Prosperity Wheel and the type you choose is entirely up to you.

You can create a Prosperity Wheel for any number of reasons. The following are some examples of specific a Prosperity Wheels:

- A Gratitude Board: This would include all the things that you are currently grateful for

- A Love Board: This could be centred around a specific personal relationship, or the relationship you have with all your family and friends

- A Money Board: This would include anything relating to finance or material wealth. It may include images of a house, car, clothing or any other material goods you want

- A Habit Board: If you're full of good intentions that never turn into reality you might like to create a Habit Board. This would include all the healthy habits you would like to incorporate into your life. For example, meditation, eating healthy foods, yoga, or regular exercise. Don't include any habits you want to break though

- A Travel Board: This may include all or some of the places in the World that you would like to visit

- A Bucket List Board: This would include all the things you want to do before you kick the bucket

Alternatively, you might just like to create a Prosperity Wheel that captures all your desires.

There are three types of Prosperity Wheel (Vision Board); each with its own purpose. These are - the 'Opening and Allowing' Prosperity

Wheel, the 'I Know Exactly What I Want' Prosperity Wheel and the 'Theme' Prosperity Wheel.

It really doesn't matter which type of Prosperity Wheel you choose. If your desires or aspirations change you can abandon the wheel and create a new one at any time. Alternatively, you can create several different Prosperity Wheels and use them concurrently. The choice is yours.

To help you to decide the right one for you I have included a brief description of each type of Prosperity Wheel. In reality, most Prosperity Wheels are a combination of all three types, but you may like to focus on one in particular.

Sometimes you'll start out doing one kind of Prosperity Wheel, and then your intuition takes over and moves you into a different mode. This is normal; it's just your creativity at work.

Also, your desires and aspirations might change as you're making your Prosperity Wheel. This is also normal, so just relax and go with what your intuition is telling you. This is simply your Higher Self guiding you.

Note: For those who are wondering who or what your Higher Self is I have included a section in the next chapter. I hope the explanation doesn't sound too fanciful and put you off prosperity work.

The following is a brief explanation of each type of Prosperity Wheel (Vision Board). Use this to help you to decide which style is right for you:

## 2.2 The Opening and Allowing Prosperity Wheel

This is the most common style of Prosperity Wheel. It is sometimes referred to as the hotchpotch or hodgepodge Prosperity Wheel. It can be used to include as many different aspirations as you choose.

You're only limited by the space on the board. Create this type of Prosperity Wheel if:

1. You're not sure exactly what you want

2. You want to ask for a variety of different things

3. You've been in a period of depression or grief and need some help focusing on the way forward

4. You have some idea of what you want but need some help to anchor it

5. You have been through a life changing experience and feel slightly adrift as a result of it

6. You want to create a Bucket List board

## 2.3 The I Know Exactly What I Want Prosperity Wheel

This style of Prosperity Wheel is helpful if you have a specific goal or aspiration in mind. This type of prosperity wheel generally focuses on just a few specific goals e.g. starting a family and finding a suitable family home. Create this type of Prosperity Wheel if:

1. You're very clear about your current desires and aspirations

2. You want to change your environment or surroundings, and know exactly what you have in mind

3. There are specific things you want to manifest in your life (e.g. a new home, starting a business, or having a baby to name just a few)

In the case of a new home, you may have the exact house in mind. Alternatively, you may have a clear picture in your mind of the type of house and its location.

## 2.4 The Themed Prosperity Wheel

This style of Prosperity Wheel is helpful if you're starting a new cycle. Create this type of Prosperity Wheel if:

1. It's your birthday or New Year's Eve or some significant event that starts a new cycle in your life

2. If you are working on one particular area of your life e.g. career or relationships

The only difference between this Prosperity Wheel and the other two is that this one has clear parameters and intent. Before you begin this Prosperity Wheel, take a moment to hold the intent and the theme in mind. When you choose pictures, they will be aligned to your chosen theme.

If you choose the 'Theme' Prosperity Wheel all your pictures will relate to the same goal. For example, if your theme is a new job all your pictures will be connected to this new role. This may include the environment, clothing, car (if a car is included with the job) or anything else you can think of.

Remember, you might start out planning one kind of Prosperity Wheel, but end up doing something different. This is OK; it's just your Higher Self connecting with you and guiding you.

Some people get confused about how they should feel while making their Prosperity Wheel and get upset if they don't feel 'spiritual'. Some may want to give up because doubt creeps in. This is quite normal. Simply acknowledge your feelings and then carry on. After all, what have you got to lose?

Your Prosperity Wheel is only limited by the extent of your own creativity. It can be very sparse or have no free space. It's important that whatever you create feels right for you.

You can change your pictures as often as you like. You may change them as they become real or as you realise you no longer need them.

When you've had enough of looking at the wheel, take it down and dismantle it or throw it away and make another one. Don't be surprised if it goes on working long after it has been taken down though. This sometimes happens.

# 3. Things You Need to Know

There are a few things that you need to know, but they don't fit into the other chapters. In this chapter I have covered the Higher Self, the power of Prosperity Wheels, money and a few words of caution.

## 3.1 Your Higher Self

When we talk about our Higher Self, it tends to conjure up images of some kind of angelic, mystical being located in some far-away place. In reality, our Higher Self is who each of us is at a deep spiritual level.

The state of your Higher Self Consciousness may be difficult to understand in words since the Higher Self is beyond the thinking mind. To connect with, and experience, your Higher Self your conscious mind must be completely silent.

This means no internal dialogue or mind chatter, which can be hard to achieve sometimes. Through deep meditation you can learn to still your conscious mind to allow communication with your Higher Self.

Your Higher Self communicates with you in various ways, including intuition, hunches and sudden unexpected life changes to name just a few. Next time you 'have a feeling' about something you will know this is your Higher Self talking to you.

In essence, it is your physical self that is the 'receiver' of these messages. It's a bit like receiving an email, telephone call, letter or text message, only it's from your Higher Self. You may or may not choose to listen or act on these communications.

If you choose to receive and follow the guidance, the potential is that you could become the physical manifestation of your Divine Self. If not, then the opposite is true. It's up to you whether you choose to accept and follow the divine guidance from your Higher Self.

In order to understand your Higher Self's function, it is important to know one very important concept. Each of us has a blueprint; a kind of 'divine template' that holds a tremendous amount of information. This blueprint exists in every atom of our beings, physical and energetic.

The amount of information that this blueprint carries is phenomenal, covering every aspect of who you are, what you are doing here, every lifetime you've ever experienced, as well as all 'potentialities' of what you are meant to become.

The main function of your Higher Self is to help you gain access to the information that resides within this blueprint. The answer to any question you could ever have could be answered by your Higher Self if you know how to hear and accept these messages.

Every problem can be solved and every obstacle can be overcome. Your Higher Self is your inner voice, spirit guide, best friend, mother, father, tour guide, entertainment director, and so much more. All of this rolled into to one very magnificent Divining Angel. Your Higher Self is not only part of you; it is at the core of your being.

You only need to become aware of your Higher Self and ask for assistance. For me, this is a mind blowing concept, but fascinating none the less.

When you create a Prosperity Wheel you're making a connection with your Higher Self. I would never suggest this is the only, or strongest, way to make a connection, but it is a connection nonetheless.

"Whatever we are waiting for - peace of mind, contentment, grace, the inner awareness of simple abundance - it will surely come to us, but only when we are ready to receive it with an open and grateful heart" - Sarah Ban Breathnach (author of Simple Abundance and the founder of the Simple Abundance Charitable Fund).

## 3.2 The Power of Prosperity Wheels

I've included the following examples to highlight the power of the Universe, not to scare you out of creating a Prosperity Wheel.

Prosperity Wheels actually work. If you put something on one that you don't really want you can end up with a problem. Equally, by putting something on your Prosperity Wheel you may get just what you want.

The stories of successful and happy outcomes of Prosperity Wheels far outweigh the mistakes. Look at the internet or read books and see many examples of new confidence, financial windfalls and babies. Examples also include new jobs, homes and great relationships, from prosperity students who made a wheel.

One of my own success stories relates to a large contract I secured for my business in 2007. A large local employer invited several training providers to submit a tender for a series of bespoke training courses. This extensive programme of training courses was to be delivered to all directors, managers and staff. We submitted our tender and then discovered that we were competing against at least two national training providers.

On my Prosperity Wheel I put the client's logo and wrote an affirmation to the Universe. My affirmation stated that this would be a win/win outcome. I said that we would win this contract and deliver a very successful programme for the client that met their needs.

Three months later we won the contract. This contract provided us with several days' work, each week for nine months. That contract amounted to 85% of our turnover that year. The client was happy and recommended us to other businesses, and so we had a win/win outcome.

A client of mine created a Prosperity Wheel around a financial theme. Her aspiration was to have wealth beyond her wildest dreams. Sure enough she accumulated the wealth that she so desperately wanted.

Unfortunately, she only focused on the financial gain and failed to include her husband as part of her plan. Their relationship didn't survive and the wealth that she had thought was so important seemed hollow without her husband to share it with her.

She should have asked for the wealth but made sure her affirmations talked about them enjoying the wealth together. She could also have made sure that some of the pictures were things they could do together. This would have told the Universe that they were both enjoying this wealth.

A friend of mine who desperately wanted a baby planned her wheel around a 'baby' theme. She told her husband about this and discovered she wasn't ready for a family as there was work to be done in their relationship first. She disposed of this Prosperity Wheel and created a new one when the time was right. If they hadn't talked about this she might have got pregnant much too early.

Another friend of mine put a picture of herself holding her baby niece. Her intention was to indicate to the Universe that she wanted to be a part of this lovely baby's life, but she obviously didn't make that clear to the Universe.

A few months later she found herself pregnant even though she was taking contraception. The message that she had put out to the Universe was that she wanted to hold a baby, and sure enough it was delivered!

Some things on your wheel will happen swiftly; almost as if they were waiting your permission to manifest. Others take more time - maybe even up to a year, or more. Don't lose heart - they will happen when the time is right. They can only come when your subconscious mind can accept that you deserve them.

"The positive thinker sees the invisible, feels the intangible, and achieves the impossible" - Author unknown

## 3.3 Money

Don't feel guilty about including money or wealth in your Prosperity Wheel. Money is important to our existence, and is simply another form of energy. It's difficult to survive without money.

"It's a kind of spiritual snobbery that makes people think they can be happy without money" - Albert Camus (French author, journalist, and philosopher).

It's important to have the right attitude to money. A question for you - if you have money but no peace or joy in your life can you really be prosperous? I don't think so! Money alone will not make you prosperous. It's all about getting the balance right.

If your financial aspirations are small then make this clear in your Prosperity Wheel. Perhaps you just want enough money to pay the bills. If so, find pictures of someone paying bills or receiving a cheque and tell the Universe this is what you want.

If however, you have big financial aspirations then tell the Universe what you want. Do you have a house in mind, or want expensive holidays, a new car or money to pay your children's school fees?

The Universe doesn't judge us; it simply tries to deliver what we ask for. Our results are often based on the clarity of our message (cosmic order) to the Universe, so be as specific as possible.

Note: don't expect your Prosperity Wheel to be a 'get rich quick' scheme. You may just be lucky enough for this to happen, but generally it doesn't work that way. The Universe will do its best for you, but not everyone can be a millionaire.

"To attract money, you must focus on wealth. It is impossible to bring more money into your life when you are noticing you do not have enough, because that means you are thinking thoughts that you do not have enough" - Rhonda Byrne (author of The Secret)

There are just a couple of rules regarding money. The first rule is make sure you ask for 'good energy money'. Ensure your request doesn't involve harming someone else in order to give you the money you desire.

The second rule is 'pay your bills with great thanks'. If you feel resentment every time you have to pay a bill, the money will come back to you even slower. If you pay with love and joyfulness, you open the free flowing channel of abundance.

A bill is an acknowledgment of your ability to pay. Someone gives you the product or the service first, entrusting you to pay. So pay each bill with thanks and appreciation. Simply tell the Universe that you will always have enough money to pay your bills. It's important to truly believe this.

"Money is like any other relationship; it comes where it's invited and appreciated. It rarely comes when it's chased." - Morgana Rae (named one of 2012's Top Women in E-commerce by WE Magazine and author of Financial Alchemy).

## 3.4 A Few Words of Caution

Before we go any further; a few words of caution.

We've all heard the expression 'be careful what you ask for - you might get it'. This is particularly true when you declare your aspirations and desires to the Universe. A Prosperity Wheel is a very powerful thing and it needs to be made and used with respect.

"Our deepest wishes are whispers of our authentic selves. We must learn to respect them. We must learn to listen" - Sarah Ban Breathnach (author of Simple Abundance and the founder of the Simple Abundance Charitable Fund)

It is vital that you ask for things for the highest good. Otherwise you are practising magic rather than spirituality and the consequences for you and others could be unpleasant.

Be very careful that you only ask for what you truly want and consider the consequences of what you're asking for. The Universe doesn't have a sense of humour so you may get exactly what you asked for and find you don't like it!

Don't go crazy and put up a picture of a famous person and ask for them to be the new relationship in your life. Instead use their picture to denote the type of looks that you like. Just make it clear in your link to the picture that it's the **type** you're after, not the actual person.

Never ask for a relationship with a married man or woman, or someone who is already in a relationship. Even if you are in love with this person your action will create bad Karma. Remember, if they can leave someone else for you then equally they can leave you for someone else.

Only ask for things you truly want. Asking for something that you don't truly want may be costly but even worse you would find that it's all been for nothing.

Ask for yourself only. Never ask for things that don't concern you e.g. World peace or an end to World poverty. You may only represent your own life on your Prosperity Wheel.

If World peace is one of your desires then tell the Universe that you want to contribute to this. You will need to tell the Universe how you plan to contribute.

"We make a living by what we get, but we make a life by what we give" - Sir Winston Churchill (British politician and statesman known for his leadership of the UK during the Second World War)

Don't be tempted to ask for exam success for your children. Instead encourage your children to create their own Prosperity Wheel. Asking for things for your children is interfering with their energy.

You can put up pictures of loved ones affirming love and happiness between you because that is part of your own life. However, making a Prosperity Wheel for someone else without their permission is interference in their life, of the highest order. You may be asking for things for someone else that doesn't matter to them.

You may have a loved one or friend who is sick and you want to picture them surrounded by health and love and light. Although this is a lovely gesture, and done with honourable intention, you still need to get their permission first. The only exception is if your spouse or your children are too sick to help themselves or give their consent.

Unless your partner/spouse is 100% with you in prosperity work don't put a joint picture on your wheel. If you do, then their energy will pull against yours and the wheel almost certainly won't work.

Note: any negative thoughts you have could prevent you achieving your aspirations so try to dispel any negative thoughts. For example, you may have a property that you would like to live in, but keep telling yourself it will never happen. If you don't believe, it probably won't happen for you.

"I choose the path of trust. I understand that I have little control in the external world. But I do have control of my reactions to it all" - Susan Jeffers (author of Feel the Fear and Do It Anyway, End the Struggle and Dance With Life and Embracing Uncertainty)

# 4. Preparation

As with any prosperity work it's important to be properly prepared before you start. The preparation stage for creating a Prosperity Wheel involves gathering the necessary supplies and identifying what's important to you.

It's also important that you're in the right state of mind to be at your most creative. This is best achieved by going through a short ritual. In case you don't have your own clarity ritual I have suggested one later in this chapter.

## 4.1 Supplies

Like all creative projects you will need a few essential supplies to complete the task. To create a Prosperity Wheel you will need the following:

- A large piece of poster board or thick paper; preferably coloured (more about the colour in the next chapter). Strong colours make a stronger impression on the mind and the Universe

- A recent photograph of you; preferably one with you smiling and looking happy and relaxed

- A large assortment of magazines (old magazines are fine for this exercise). Make sure you find lots of different magazines. If you limit your options you'll stifle your creativity

- Clip art, drawings or photographs

- Internet access may be helpful if you can't find the images, words or phrases you want in the magazines

- Glue

- Scissors

- A pen to write your affirmations (A medium marker pen is ideal for this task)

- Music (play some music that you like, and that makes you feel good. Don't play music that makes you feel depressed or sad)

## 4.2 Your aspirations/desires

It's important to tell the Universe what you want. If your pictures or affirmations clearly state what you want the Universe will find it much easier to help you achieve your desired outcomes.

For example, several weeks ago I added picture of a song thrush to my Prosperity Wheel because I hadn't seen any in our garden for some time. This morning a song thrush was feeding on our lawn. Was it purely coincidence or synchronicity?

If you're struggling to get started don't panic. You might find it helpful to ask yourself the following questions:

1. What will you do differently when you realise your goal?

2. Where would you travel if money wasn't an issue?

3. Where would you live? Try to be specific about the town, county or country

4. What would you wear? Do you dream about wearing designer clothes and shoes? Don't ask this question if you're really not interested in clothes or shoes

5. What material goods would you own e.g. a boat, sports car, caravan, or anything else you can think of?

6. What kind of vehicle would you drive? For example, are you hankering for a sports car, a 4x4 or a Harley Davidson motorbike?

7. What would you do for work? Would you work?

8. Who would you help? This may be voluntary work or help you would offer to family and friends

9. What would you do with your leisure time or me time?

This list isn't conclusive. Hopefully it provides you with a starting point if you need a helping hand to get started.

In my experience most people's aspirations fall into the following categories - health, wealth, family and friends, career or job, leisure time and hobbies, relationships, personal space and spirituality or beliefs.

**Health:** do you enjoy good health and want this to continue? Or, do you currently suffer with ill health and would like help to heal?

**Wealth:** think about what wealth means to you. It's different for each of us. Is it about paying the bills, a luxury lifestyle, or something in between?

**Family and friends:** do you want closer ties and more time together? Do you want to heal a rift? Do you simply want things to continue as they are as you're happy with your family and friends relationships?

**Career or job:** do you have a dream job that you would love to do? Are you unemployed and looking for work? Have you always wanted to have a go at being self-employed? Would you like to take early retirement or voluntary redundancy?

**Leisure time and hobbies:** Are you happy with how you spend your leisure time, or are there things you really want to do? Have you always dreamed of learning to ride a horse like a professional, or learning to fly?

**Relationships:** are you looking for Mr/Miss Right? Are you in a happy relationship but want to get married? Is there a relationship that needs to be terminated?

**Personal space:** do you have as much 'me time' as you desire, or would you like more 'me time'? What would you like to do with your 'me time'? Do you simply want me time to read a book or time to go to the gym? Perhaps you would simply like some uninterrupted 'me time'

**Spirituality or beliefs:** for some this is about religion. For others spirituality and beliefs means something else. Have you always wanted to explore another religion? Have you always wanted to attend a Buddhist retreat? The list is endless

Your desires don't have to fall into these categories. Like the nine questions above, these are just ideas to give you a starting point. You may have totally different aspirations that don't come under any of these headings.

As part of your preparation ritual ask yourself which aspects of your life are important to you now. With luck the answers will come to you.

Just visualise or feel what you want. Don't worry about how the Universe will manifest these things for you. Your role is to request and believe; the Universe is responsible for delivering.

Expect your aspirations to change over time. This is a living document and so the pictures that mean something to you today may not in 12 months' time. You may even change your mind about what you want as you start looking through the magazines.

"Life is a field of unlimited possibilities" - Deepak Chopra (Indian-born, American physician, author and one of the pre-eminent leaders of the mind-body-spirit movement).

## 4.3 A Simple Clarity Ritual

In order to be at you most creative you need to be in a relaxed state and have an open mind so that your Higher Self can talk to you.

I recommend that you create a ritual before you begin your Prosperity Wheel (or any other prosperity work). Even if you are doing prosperity work as part of a group activity, take a little time before you start flicking through the magazines and cutting out pictures.

I have been using the following simple clarity ritual for many years for my own prosperity work and when working with my clients. Please feel free to use this clarity ritual or create your own.

**Step 1:** Put on soft music. Don't select high energy or loud music, or music that makes you think about the words. For each of us the right music will be different, and you may work through several pieces of music before you find the right one.

**Step 2:** Light a candle. Lighting a candle for a particular purpose or intention is practiced worldwide, by people of all walks of life. Lighting a candle symbolises bringing light to your wishes or desires.

**Step 3:** Sit quietly, lose yourself in the music and set the intention i.e. connect with your Higher Self. This can be as simple as asking your Higher Self to guide you to select the right pictures.

**Step 4:** With lots of kindness and openness, ask your Higher Self what you **truly** want. You may hear a word or words. Maybe images will come into your head. Just take a few moments to reflect on what's important to you.

During the simple clarity ritual, and while you are making your Prosperity Wheel, you may experience internal dialogue/mind chatter running through your head. Just acknowledge these thoughts and then let them go, and keep on working!

Don't feel the need to rush this clarity ritual as you will have plenty of time to create the right Prosperity Wheel for you. Just allow your conscious mind to accept whatever you hear, feel or see.

When you feel ready you can start the process of creating your Prosperity Wheel.

"The only place opportunity cannot be found is in a closed-minded person" - Bo Bennett (American business man, author, philanthropist and motivational speaker)

# 5. Creating a Prosperity Wheel

Creating your personal Prosperity Wheel involves selecting the right pictures and writing affirmations that make your desires clear. Remember, only select images of what you want and write affirmations that suggest you already have it.

If you include things you don't want you'll get them too. I know I've made this point several times in the book, but you won't believe how many people include things they want to rid themselves of.

## 5.1 Pictures for Your Prosperity Wheel

If you are going to create the **'Opening and Allowing'** Prosperity Wheel go through each magazine and cut out the pictures that delight you. Don't ask why. Just keep going through the magazines.

If it's a picture of a teddy bear that makes you smile, then cut it out. Equally, if it's a country cottage, a windmill or a town house you like then cut it out.

It doesn't matter what the picture is, what it means to you or why you want to keep it; simply cut it out and put in the pile for now. You will sort the pictures later.

This type of Prosperity Wheel can have many different goals.

If you are going to create the **'I Know Exactly What I Want'** Prosperity Wheel then you have a clear desire (or desires) in mind. In this case go through each magazine and cut out the pictures that fit your vision.

This type of Prosperity Wheel usually has more than one goal but not as many as the Opening and Allowing Prosperity Wheel. For example, perhaps you want a smallholding in the country and want to study for a degree. In this case your pictures will focus on both of these desires.

If you want a house by the water, then look at a home-style magazines or search Estate Agents websites for the exact house (or something similar).

If you want to start your own business, find images that capture that your business idea. If you want to learn to play a musical instrument then find a picture of someone playing the instrument you're interested in, and so on.

If you plan to create the **'Theme'** Prosperity Wheel go through each magazine and cut out the pictures that link to the theme in some way. For example, if you want to create a Prosperity Wheel for your wedding choose pictures relating to the dress, venue, honeymoon destination, food, wedding cake and anything else you can think of.

The theme Prosperity Wheel generally has one overarching topic and every picture relates to it. You will end up with a collage of pictures that all relate to the same goal in some way.

## 5.2 Affirmations for Your Prosperity Wheel

It really is very important to ensure you are making positive statements that suggest you already have the things you are dreaming of. Don't write something like 'I hope to have/be' or 'I would like'.

Remember how literal the Universe gets—if you want something now, you have to inform the Universe that it is already planning to send it to you.

It's fine to set long-term goals but you need to tell the Universe when you want it to manifest. For example, you might want to retire in 2015. If so, your affirmation might be "By the end of 2015 I will retire and have plenty of money for my retirement."

There are no right or wrong affirmations as this is your personal message to the Universe. In case you're struggling to come up with the right affirmations for your Prosperity Wheel I've included some suggestions to get you started.

## Health
- I enjoy good physical health and emotional wellbeing
- Thank you for my healthy body
- I am the healthiest I have ever been
- I am in excellent physical and mental health
- My health, strength and fitness are at optimum levels, I look and feel great
- I am perfectly healthy in body, mind and spirit
- I radiate good health

## Relationships
- We have a strong and loving relationship (include a picture of you and your loved one together)
- I am enjoying the best relationship ever
- I am very happy and grateful that [name] and I found each other, and have a very blessed relationship
- I am living my perfect life with my perfect partner, who is a friend, lover and soul mate
- Thank you universe for bringing [name] into my life. My life is now complete with this beautiful human being
- I have a lovely family and great friends
- I am enjoying quality time with my family and friends

## Financial
- Everyone who receives my products/services has the money and whatever else they need to purchase my products/services today
- My products/services benefits my customers and create wealth for me
- I give thanks for a quick and substantial increase in my financial income now
- My income is constantly increasing and I prosper wherever I turn
- I have plenty of money
- Money and success come to me easily
- I make plenty of money doing what I love
- Money flows to me from all directions easily and effortlessly
- My business has an annual turnover of [sum]
- I have sufficient money to buy a [name the item]
- I have the funds to pay my children's school fees/university fees

## Career
- I'm doing the job I love, and am being richly rewarded for it
- I'm doing my dream job as a [name the job]

- I will start my own business on [date]
- I am running my own successful business
- I will pass my annual appraisal/exams with flying colours

If one of your aspirations is to own a certain type of house put up a picture that looks like the house that you really want. As part of your affirmation and add the location. You might choose to add 'in the Cotswolds', 'in Devon', 'in Scotland', 'in Australia'. This will help the Universe to locate the right house for you.

If you have a timescale in mind for any of your aspirations then tell the Universe. As part of your affirmation write the date when you want this to happen. For example, I am enjoying a lovely six-week trip to Australia in July 2013.

Your job is now done so don't worry about how the Universe will manifest these things for you. The Universe will know the best and the fastest way to deliver what you want. Just believe it will happen.

On her website Susan Jeffers is offering a free booklet on affirmations, called Why Affirmations Are So Powerful! Simply visit her website and follow the link.

"If you see yourself as prosperous, you will be. If you see yourself as continually hard up, that is exactly what you will be" - Robert Collier (American author of self-help books)

## 5.3 Steps-by-Step Guide to Creating Your Prosperity Wheel

Now that you're properly prepared it's time to begin making the collage that will be your new Prosperity Wheel. It's important to focus on what you truly want. Choose your pictures and affirmations carefully.

Your subconscious mind works in pictures and images so make your wheel as big, bright and colourful as possible. Drab small images bring drab and small results! A2 card/paper is an ideal size for your Prosperity Wheel. Most stationers and craft shops stock card and paper in a variety of colours in this size.

Try to avoid black and white pictures as they don't work well in creative visualisation. Your Prosperity Wheel can include pictures from magazines, drawings or clip art, or a combination of them all. The choice is yours.

You may also select words or phrases for your Prosperity Wheel. One of the phrases on my Prosperity Wheel is 'In good health' because I am in good health and want to stay this way.

Each picture on your Prosperity Wheel should evoke a positive emotional response from you. The mere sight of your Prosperity Wheel should make you happy and fuel your passion to achieve it every time you look at it. If this doesn't happen change your pictures.

Catherine Ponder suggests specific colour schemes depending on what you want to manifest. If you know what you want, or have a theme in mind you might like to use one of the following colours for your Prosperity Wheel:

- Green or gold for money (all things financial), jobs and career success

- Yellow or white for spiritual understanding and development

- Blue (any shade) for education, intellect, writing books or articles, or studying for a degree

- Yellow or orange for health and energy

- Pink or warm red for love, romance, marriage, or happiness in human relationships

You may feel drawn to pink or red as a colour, but not be planning to focus on romance in your Prosperity Wheel. This is fine; it's just your Higher Self guiding you towards a colour that works for you.

If you're not sure which colour you want to use I recommend you choose gold coloured card or paper. Gold is an excellent prosperity colour. Gold is the colour of riches and so works well for all forms of prosperity, good luck, money, vitality, health and success.

**Step 1:** choose your background colour
Choose the background colour that you feel most connected with.

**Step 2:** the Universal Disclaimer
Write the all-important Universal Disclaimer at the top of your wheel - **'These things or better now manifest for me in easy and pleasant ways for the highest good of all concerned'.** This disclaimer should always be added to your Prosperity Wheel as it's important that you wish for 'the highest good of all concerned'.

Note: it is important to include this Universal Disclaimer on your board so that you don't get the cash for your new sports car through a court case, insurance claim (as a result of personal injury), or through any means that will hurt someone else.

At the bottom of your wheel write **'I am worthy of the best the Universe can offer'** (and believe it!)

**Step 3:** add your photo
Paste a lovely photo of yourself in the centre of the board. By placing your photograph in the centre of the board you're making it clear to the Universe that you're at the heart of this wheel. It also tells the Universe that each picture relates to you, your life and your aspirations.

Of course you can create a Prosperity Wheel without including your photograph, but your picture strengthens the intent. It's a bit like giving the Universe a helping hand.

**Step 4:** choose your style of Prosperity Wheel
If you don't already know which type of Prosperity Wheel you want to create choose one now. It's OK to change your mind as you go through the magazines but it's helpful to have a style in mind at this stage. If in doubt, opt for the 'Opening and Allowing' Prosperity Wheel.

One of my clients decided to create a Prosperity Wheel for the New Year. Her theme was to be the 'big goals' she wanted to achieve in the coming year. As she was sorting her pictures she realised her theme was about her everyday life and not big goals at all.

She was both surprised and delighted because she realised that the 'big goals' didn't matter as much to her as creating a daily life of happiness.

**Step 5:** select your pictures, phrases and words
Go through your magazines and cut out the pictures, words or headlines that appeal to you. Don't question why. No gluing yet! Let yourself have fun looking through the magazines. It's important to have fun and not put any time constraints on yourself.

Make a big pile of images, phrases and words, but don't go back to them until you have finished going through all the magazines. The sifting phase comes later. It's OK to choose similar pictures because you will eliminate the ones you don't want later.

Keep going through this process until you have looked through each magazine or you instinctively feel you don't need to carry on searching any more. You can go through the magazines as many times as you want to.

If you can't find the pictures you want you can search the internet for images, words or phrases, or even draw your own. There are no rules when it comes to selecting the right pictures for your Prosperity Wheel.

**Step 6:** sort your pictures and clippings
Sort through the images and begin to lay your favourites in a new pile. Sorting is all about trusting your intuition.

As you sort through your pile of pictures some may not feel right, or may no longer capture your imagination because you've found better pictures. You may discover that what you thought was important isn't any more. Trust yourself enough to eliminate them.

As you look at these images and your spirit gets quieter your ego tends to drift away and loosen its grip. When this happens your High Self is able to take control and help you to select the right images for you.

Dispose of the pictures, words or phrases that you've eliminated so you don't end up accidentally including them in your Prosperity Wheel.

Next, take each picture in turn and ask yourself what this picture is telling you. Does it mean you need to take better care of yourself? Does it mean you want to get a dog, or stop mixing with a particular person who drains you? Does it make you feel like you want to move house or change job? The possibilities are endless.

Most likely you'll know the answer when you look at the picture. If you don't, but you still love the image, then keep it anyway. Images of flowers have this effect on me; I never know why I'm including them but every Prosperity Wheel I've ever created has flowers on it somewhere.

**Step 7:** organise your pictures
Lay the pictures on your poster board, but **don't** paste them into place yet. As you do this, you'll get a sense of how the wheel should be laid out.

For instance, you might assign a theme to each corner of the wheel e.g. Health, Business, Spirituality and Relationships. You might prefer to lay the images randomly all over the board in no particular order. You might even want to fold the board into a book that tells a story. The choice is yours and the options are endless.

Don't worry about being artistic—that's not the point of this exercise. The point is that your wheel should resonate with your emotions. Arrange your pictures in a way that gives you an emotional connection to your Prosperity Wheel.

You may find yourself moving the pictures around several times before you finally decide on the right location. Equally, you may start out creating a portrait style Prosperity Wheel but end up changing it to Landscape. Just do what feels right to you.

**Step 8:** paste
After you've arranged all the items in a way that works for you, paste everything onto your poster board. Take your time doing this, and leave enough space between your photograph and the pictures to write an affirmation for each one.

**Step 9:** affirmations and decoration

When you've finished pasting all the images onto your Prosperity Wheel it's time to write your affirmations and add any decoration that you want to include.

Draw a line to link each picture to your photograph. The lines on your Prosperity Wheel will probably look like the spokes of a wheel. These lines help strengthen the intent, by making a connection between you and each picture.

Next write your affirmation on, above or below the line. This is your message (cosmic order) to the Universe. For example, if you've included a picture of Australia your affirmation might be 'I am enjoying a lovely 6 week holiday in Australia'.

Be sure to write your 'affirmations' in the present tense. Remember how literal the Universe gets. If you want something now, you have to inform the Universe that it is already planning to send it to you.

You might also like to add some decorative touches to your poster board. You can draw or paint on it, add stickers or even add glitter. I often add hearts or stars to my Prosperity Wheels.

On the back of your Prosperity Wheel write 'Date created' followed by today's date. Also write 'Date Manifested' (leave this blank for now). This will enable you to monitor how long it took for your desires to manifest.

**Step 10:** display
Hang your Prosperity Wheel. I recommend you hang your Prosperity Wheel in a prominent place where you'll see it regularly (preferably daily) e.g. your office, sitting room, hallway, bedroom door, bedroom wall or wardrobe door.

Some prosperity teachers, like Catherine Ponder, say what is sacred is secret and so your Prosperity Wheel should be hidden away. However, most prosperity teachers believe that we should place the wheel where it can be seen regularly.

Some teach that the greatest successes come to those who make their wheel visible to others as well as themselves. They believe this enables other people to help you manifest what you want.

This is a matter of personal choice. Personally, I have my Prosperity Wheel hanging on the wall in my study so that I can look at it regularly.

**Step 11:** do something/act
I know no one likes to be told to do something, but we do need to give the Universe a helping hand. Taking conscious action in your daily life is a key component of the manifestation process.

"If you create opportunities, luck will follow" - Noel Edmonds (English entrepreneur, TV broadcaster, former Radio DJ and author of Positively Happy: Cosmic Ways to Change Your Life and Noel Edmonds - Positively Tranquil audio CD)

Taking action doesn't mean being busy or pushing yourself too hard. Taking action means being open to manifesting prosperity. It means listening to your Higher Self. It means keeping your eyes and ears open to opportunities and moving towards them.

Pay attention to your Prosperity Wheel so you can spot opportunities when they arise. Be willing to take a few chances and make the odd mistake.

"Only those who dare to fail greatly can ever achieve greatly" - Robert F Kennedy (American politician and civil rights activist)

If your wheel includes pictures of a beautiful new home, then begin to make your current home beautiful. If your home feels loved it will be easier to sell or rent to someone else so you can move on to your ideal home.

If you included pictures of healthy food, then read books about healthy eating, and be more aware of what you eat. You have to help the Universe a bit!

If you included pictures that remind you of starting a business join relevant networking groups or pay for the services of a business/life coach to help you fulfil your dreams.

"If you take one step towards your dreams, your dreams will take multiple steps towards you" - Christine Kane (American folk singer/songwriter, and keynote speaker on women's issues, creativity, and business)

For a deeper understanding about step 11 look for books and articles on the 'Law of Attraction'. There are endless books, articles and gurus focusing on this subject so it won't be hard to find further information. Simply type 'Law of Attraction' into Google or another search engine. I have also suggested some further reading in chapter 12.

Finally, look at and enjoy the pictures of what you're creating in your life. Change them as they become real or as you realise you no longer need them.

When you've had enough of looking at the wheel, take it down and dismantle it or throw it away and make another one. Don't be surprised if it goes on working long after it's been taken down.

"Imagine that the Universe is like a cosmic kitchen with an infinite menu, just waiting to take and fulfil you orders" - Patricia J Crane Ph.D. (author of Ordering from the Cosmic Kitchen: The Essential Guide to Powerful, Nourishing Affirmations).

I have included two examples of a Prosperity Wheel in this book. The first example is the 'Opening and Allowing Prosperity Wheel', and the second example is the 'Theme Prosperity Wheel'.

## 5.3.1 Example of the Opening and Allowing Prosperity Wheel

In my example I have covered a house move, health, spiritual and emotional wellbeing, travel, relationships, finance and book writing and publishing.

Each of these is important to me at present, but this will change over time. Some things will appear on each Prosperity Wheel you create. Others my only appear once.

### 5.3.2 Example of the Themed Prosperity Wheel

I have chosen the theme of work/business for my themed Prosperity Wheel. I've chosen this because my work/business activities are going through a period of significant change. So far the changes have been out of my control, but now I want to play a part in directing what I do in future.

All the images I've selected relate to my work/business aspirations in some way. I have a study/studio. I want a study to work from, but I also want a studio where I can run workshops.

I have also told the Universe that I'm a successful writer as I didn't specify this on my last Prosperity Wheel. I've been writing and publishing books for several years, but without great success. I also want to continue my work as a coach and mentor so I've included this on my Prosperity Wheel.

The Universe has already set to work on the coaching/mentoring goal. Earlier this week I was approached about being a Progression Mentor for the Prince's Trust.

Finally, I've added money to my themed Prosperity Wheel; otherwise I'm in danger of doing everything for no financial return.

"Empty pockets never held anyone back. Only empty heads and empty hearts can do that" - Dr Norman Vincent Peale (author of The Power of Positive Thinking)

# 6. Alternatives to Traditional Prosperity Wheels

The theory behind the Law of Attraction is that we create our own realities. We attract the people in our lives, our material goods, and the money in our bank accounts through our thoughts and feelings.

If your beliefs are limited, you will attract limited prosperity and abundance. As long as you truly believe anything is possible, the sky's the limit. What's more, the Law of Attraction can work in many ways.

Not everyone wants to create a traditional Prosperity Wheel. If you aren't a visual person you may find it difficult to tell the Universe what your goals and aspirations are in pictures. That's fine because you don't have to limit yourself to just a poster board and paste.

There are many ways to manifest the things you truly want. I have included some alternatives to traditional Prosperity Wheels for you. Experiment and see which works best for you. However you choose to submit your cosmic order the Universe will get the message.

Whichever method of cosmic ordering you choose always remember to include the Universal Disclaimer.

## 6.1 A Vision Journal

A Vision Journal is the same thing as a Prosperity Wheel (Vision Board). The difference is you create it on the pages of a spiral bound notebook. I recommend using a big sketch pad as bigger pictures get better results.

In a Vision Journal you can keep adding pages or tear pages out as your aspirations and desires change.

I recommend that you make it a point of looking at your Vision Journal every day, and tear out the things you no longer want or have already manifested. This helps the Universe to focus on the images pasted in the journal.

Here are a few questions to write down in your Vision Journal:

1. If fear of failure, money, other people's opinions and judgement were not factors – what would I want to be, do, or have?

2. What beliefs, or things, would I have to let go of if I were to create this in my life?

3. In order to 'be, do, or have' these things what would I have to believe?

Write the all-important Universal Disclaimer at the start of your Vision Journal - **'These things or better now manifest for me in easy and pleasant ways for the highest good of all concerned'.**

On the first page of your Vision Journal also write **'I am worthy of the best the Universe can offer'** (and believe it).

## 6.2 Magic Lists

If a Vision Journal doesn't work for you then you may prefer to try creating a series of 'Magic Lists' instead. Think of Magic Lists as a shopping list of your goals, aspirations and desires.

Create three separate lists. Write BE at the top of the first sheet. DO at the top of the second sheet, and HAVE at the top of the third sheet.

Immediately underneath the heading on each sheet write the Universal Disclaimer - **'These things or better now manifest for me in easy and pleasant ways for the highest good of all concerned'.**

At the bottom of each sheet also write **'I am worthy of the best the Universe can offer'.**

On a piece of scrap paper make lists of things you want for each of these headings. You don't have to do this in any particular order, and you can amend your list as often as you like.

When you're ready transfer these cosmic orders to your BE, DO and HAVE sheets. Write each cosmic order in the present tense (as if you already have these things). For example, 'I am happy and grateful now that................'

Your affirmation should explain, as clearly as possible, how you want your life to be. I know it can feel awkward writing affirmations that state you already have the things you desire. Writing your cosmic orders in the present tense strengthens the intent.

Read your lists out loud and then put them somewhere that you will remember to view them regularly (preferably daily). You can add to your list at any time. You can also delete items from your lists at any time.

## 6.3 Vision Poem

If your particular talent is poetry you may prefer to write your prosperity lists (also known as cosmic orders) as a beautiful poem for the Universe. Your poem can be as long or short as you like.

Describe your ideal image of yourself and your life in as much detail as possible. The clearer your message is the more accurate your manifestations will be.

Read your poem out loud and then put it into your purse, diary or anywhere else that it will be close to you. Read it regularly (preferably daily).

At the end of your poem write the Universal Disclaimer - **'These things or better now manifest for me in easy and pleasant ways for the highest good of all concerned'**. Also write **'I am worthy of the best the Universe can offer'**.

## 6.4 Digital Vision Boards

Digital Vision Boards are becoming ever more popular. There are various software programs that will create a film for your computer desktop. For example, you may choose to create a short video for 'youtube'.

In Google (or any other search engine) type 'Vision Board Software'. This will give you various options to choose from.

Personally, I'm a fan of traditional Prosperity Wheels. I like the process of selecting and organising the pictures, but a Digital Vision Board may be your preferred method.

Even if you are creating a Digital Vision Board, don't forget to include the Universal Disclaimer. At the end of your recording say - **'These things or better now manifest for me in easy and pleasant ways for the highest good of all concerned'**

Follow this up with **'I am worthy of the best the Universe can offer'**. Make sure you say the words with conviction.

## 6.5 Vision Index Cards

Vision index cards are sometimes referred to as 'Affirmation Cards' or 'Prayer Cards'.

On your first Vision Index Card write the Universal Disclaimer - **'These things or better now manifest for me in easy and pleasant ways for the highest good of all concerned.'** Underneath this write **'I am worthy of the best the Universe can offer'**. Remember to read this card regularly not just skip to the cards that hold your desires.

On the front of each card paste images that represent your ideal life. As the cards aren't very big just put one image on each card, and use the biggest picture you can find that will fit. On the back of each card write an affirmation that is relevant to the picture on the front.

You can have as many or as few cards as you like. You can keep adding cards or throwing cards away as your desires change. The choice is yours.

Every day sort through your cards and read the affirmations aloud. Some people like to focus on just one card each day; others like to focus on all of them. There are no right or wrong ways of doing this.

Note: you may like to get your cards laminated as they will quickly become dog-eared (tatty) with frequent use.

As the cards take up very little room you may choose to store them somewhere after your desires have manifested, as a reminder of the power of intention.

"If you want to change who you are, begin by changing the size of your dream. Even if you are broke, it does not cost you anything to dream of being rich. Many poor people are poor because they have given up on dreaming" - Robert Kiyosaki (Author of Rich Dad, Poor Dad)

# 7. Karmic Contract

Now that you've created your Prosperity Wheel you might like to add your own Karmic Contract (Karmic Reward) to it. If so, put your Karmic Contract on the back of your Prosperity Wheel.

If you don't accept your reward graciously you will be sending a message to the Universe that you don't feel worthy. You will find more about gratitude in chapter 9. By conveying ungratefulness or unworthiness you may well be overlooked the next time, or at the very least be sent to the back of the line for any future handouts.

"Every good thought, every good word, every good emotion, and every act of kindness, is lifting the vibration of your being to new heights. As you begin to raise your vibration, a new life and a new world will reveal itself to you" - Rhonda Byrne (author of The Secret).

With this in mind you may like to create your own Karmic Contract. Below is an example of a Karmic Contract that some of my clients use. If this works for you please feel free to use it too:

I .................................... (Your name) am now willing to release all previous vows of poverty, sacrifice, unhappiness, loneliness, sickness and struggle. Furthermore, I also give up any attachment to suffering or fear of success. I affirm that none of these qualities are of my natural state.

I .................................... (Your name) now claim my natural right to health, love, happiness and wealth. I declare that I am now manifesting all my heart's desires, easily and effortlessly, without struggle. I no longer feel the need to create suffering for myself.

I.................................... (Your name) now affirm that the Universe has been informed of these changes, and it will now begin to respond accordingly. I affirm that I am in an eternal state of perfect prosperity and peace.

This contract nullifies and voids all previous contracts to the contrary.

.................................................................................

(Signature)                                              (Date)

# 8. Creative Visualisation Success Stories

I thought it might be helpful to include a selection of success stories to help demonstrate the power of the Law of Attraction.

I have broken this chapter down into two parts. In section 8.1 I have included stories of well-known people who have successfully manifested what they want. In section 8.2 I have included the stories of ordinary people who have their own success story to tell. Each of these people has used their chosen method of creative visualisation; not necessarily a Prosperity Wheel.

I hope my selection helps inspire you to experiment with your own Prosperity Wheel or other methods of manifestation.

## 8.1 Famous People Success Stories

I have taken a small selection of examples from famous people who have used creative visualisation techniques to activate the Law of Attraction in their lives.

**John Assaraf** is a successful entrepreneur and author, and his is a real rags to riches story.

John Assaraf brought the age-old concept of a Vision Board (Prosperity Wheel) into the public eye by telling his story in 'The Secret'.

John tells the story about an incident that occurred in May 2000. He was working in his home office in his beautiful new home in Southern California. His five-year old son came in and asked him what was in the dusty boxes in the corner of his home office.

John told him that they contained his Vision Boards. His son didn't understand what they were, so John opened one of the boxes to show him. When John pulled out the second board from the box, he began to cry.

On this Vision Board was a picture of a 7,000 square foot house on top of six acres of spectacular land. John had seen this picture in the Dream Homes magazine in 1995. He had cut the picture out and stuck it on his Vision Board.

This was the exact house that he had just purchased several weeks earlier. In John's words this was a sure testament to the Law of Attraction at work.

"We can have whatever it is we choose, I don't care how big it is" - John Assaraf

**Bruce Lee**, the late martial arts legend and actor, also understood the power of the Law of Attraction. As a struggling entrepreneur and actor, Bruce sat down one day and wrote the following letter to himself:

"By 1980, I will be the best known oriental movie star in the United States, and will have secured $10 million dollars... And in return, I will give the very best acting I could possibly give every single time I am in front of the camera and I will live in peace and harmony."

In 1973, months after Bruce Lee's untimely death, Enter the Dragon (his blockbuster film) was released in both the United States and China. This elevated Bruce Lee to the level of an international star.

According to Jack Canfield (co-creator of the Chicken Soup for the Soul book series) the letter that Bruce Lee wrote to himself is hanging up on one of the walls at Planet Hollywood in New York City.

"As you think, so shall you become" - Bruce Lee

**Jim Carrey** is a Canadian and American actor, comedian, and film producer. He also shares his testament to the Law of Attraction at work.

As a struggling young comedian trying to make it in Hollywood, Jim Carrey was just about ready to give up his dream of becoming a professional actor and comedian. He had just performed at an open mic session at one of the nightclubs in Los Angeles and had been booed off the stage by his audience.

He sat down, alone, at the top of Mulholand Drive and looked out at the city below him (the city that held his future success or failure).

He then pulled out his chequebook and wrote himself a cheque for $10 million dollars and wrote the following note on it: 'for acting services rendered.'

He then carried that cheque with him in his wallet everywhere he went from that day forward. By 1995, after the success of Ace Ventura: Pet Detective, Dumb and Dumber, and The Mask, his contract price had risen to $20 million dollars.

"It is better to risk starving to death then surrender. If you give up on your dreams, what's left?" - Jim Carrey

**Noel Edmonds** is an English TV broadcaster, former Radio DJ and author of Positively Happy: Cosmic Ways to Change Your Life and Noel Edmonds - Positively Tranquil audio CD.

In 1968 Noel Edmonds was offered a place at the University of Surrey but he turned it down in favour of a job as a newsreader on Radio Luxembourg. From there he went onto have a successful British radio and TV career for many years.

His TV career ended with 'Noel's House Party' in 1999. In 2004 a TV documentary called 'The Curse of Noel Edmonds' tracing the rise and fall of his showbiz career was aired. At this time he was not in the public eye.

In Noel's own words "It wasn't until I read Barbel Mohr's book on cosmic ordering that I realised I was a positive person. That's why, in all those years after the BBC ungratefully dumped me after my fantastic successes with Swap Shop and Noel's House Party, and while my second marriage was breaking up, I never doubted I would be back one day."

Noel says that when he first started in radio he had a dream of owning a helicopter and racing powerboats, and now he does both.

Following the documentary 'The Curse of Noel Edmonds' he stated that one of his wishes was for a new challenge. Later he was offered the chance to return to TV to work on Deal or No Deal.

He later went on to write his own book titled 'Positively Happy: Cosmic Ways to Change Your Life'.

Noel Edmonds has just married for the third time, and claims this time he has met his soul mate. Friends of his say it was as a result of a cosmic order that he placed. His friends say he put in an order to find the love of his life – and months later she appeared.

'"Throughout the many ups and downs, the successes and the failures in my life, there has been a consistent and all-embracing belief that a positive attitude produces results" - Noel Edmonds

**Loral Langemeier** is Founder and CEO of Live Out Loud. She is also the author of Put More Cash in Your Pocket: Turn What You Know into Dough, The Millionaire Maker: Act, Think, and Make Money the Way the Wealthy Do, Yes! Energy: The Equation to Do Less, Make More, The Millionaire Maker's Guide to Creating a Cash Machine for Life and The Millionaire Maker's Guide to Wealth Cycle Investing: Build Your Assets Into a Lifetime of Financial Freedom.

Loral Langemeier is a true American success story. She did not start out life with money or connections. Rather than realize her obstacles in life, she focused on the possibilities.

Loral had life-long plan to be millionaire by the age of 35. She reached that goal two weeks shy of her 34th birthday. Her portfolio at that time contained real estate properties, businesses, gas/oil, and notes.

Today she is recognised as one of the World's most visible and innovative money experts.

"I grew up on, you have to work hard for money, you have to work hard for money. And so I replaced that with, Money comes easily and frequently. Now in the beginning it feels like a lie, right? There's was a part of your brain, that will say, 'Oh you liar, it's hard.' So, you have to know this little tennis match that will go on for a while" - Loral Langemeier

**Lisa Nichols** is one of the featured teachers of The Secret and co-author of the Chicken Soup for the Soul Series. She is also the Founder and CEO of Motivating the Teen Spirit.

Lisa Nichols was abused as a child and abused as an adult. By developing and toning her own bounce-back muscles at critical points in her life, Lisa found the power to become her authentic self and achieve everything she dared to hope for. She has now published her survival techniques in 'No Matter What: 9 Steps to Living the Life You Love.' She also enjoys a very successful career and is in constant demand for public speaking engagements.

"Whatever you may be going through, the darkness is only temporary—it's not your destiny" - Lisa Nichols

Other famous people who have successfully harnessed the Law of Attraction include:

- Andrew Carnegie (Carnegie Hall is named after him)
- Napoleon Hill (author of Think and Grow Rich)
- Henry Ford (Founder of the Ford Motor Company)
- Jack Canfield (author of Chicken Soup For the Soul)
- John Gray (author of Men are from Mars, Women are from Venus)

I'm sure there are many more people who have their own visualisation success stories to tell. You might like to undertake your own research.

## 8.2 Success Stories From Ordinary People

The stories in this section are not about the rich and famous. Instead, these are ordinary people who happen to have manifested the things they want in their life, and were happy to share their story.

**Kathy's Story:** I've had an extreme life change this year. In the last 12 months I have divorced, dropped to my lowest point and met my new soul mate.

A few months ago I told my children my list of requirements for a new life partner. They laughed and told me that I had better get ready to grow old alone as the list was too stringent. I just smiled and said I believe 100% that the right man is out there, waiting for me.

My requirements were - truthful, loyal, affectionate, grateful, positive, clean, Christian, supportive and trustworthy. John is all of these.

It's early days but I do believe I have met him! Why do I believe this? Easy; I asked, I believed and now I have received.

**Richard's Story:** I had been doing the same job for 5 years without moving upwards. I didn't even get the chance to try anything new in the company.

I resigned myself to not getting a promotion but I asked the Universe for a pay rise. Within a month I got a double surprise. I was offered a new job in the company and got a rise that was two steps above what I asked for.

I wish I'd placed my cosmic order sooner!

**Mandeep's Story:** I have always wanted to win the Euro millions Jackpot. I kept buying lottery tickets but nothing happened.

Then I started reading about the Law of Attraction and other people's stories. I made notes on what mistakes I was making.

I chose my goal, visualised and believed that I had already won. I bought the ticket with the 100% believe that I had already won this jackpot and was just fulfilling the formality. I checked my ticket, I was in tears as all of my 5 numbers and 2 stars matched and I was the actual winner of that jackpot.

**Sarah's Story:** After reading The Secret, I decided to create a Prosperity Wheel. I put images of places I'd like to visit and the person I saw myself being in a few years.

I meditated on it for a few weeks and put it up on my bedroom wall. Several months later, I offered the chance to go to Mexico.

I did so many amazing things Mexico. It wasn't until months later I looked at the board and realised that one of the pictures was of the Arc in Cabo San Lucas. This place was on my Prosperity Wheel and I had no idea.

**Kay's Story:** On my birthday I made a decision that I would no longer settle for anything less than my soul mate. I set an intention that I was going to meet him over the next twelve months, before my 40th birthday.

I enlisted the help of my best friends. I gave them permission to challenge me if I was doing anything to distract myself or that wasn't in my highest and best interest. My aim was to meet 'the one'.

I wrote a 'spec' describing in detail what my future husband would be like. I put my wish list in a beautiful box that I call my magical creation box.

As part of my intention-setting I signed up to an online dating service. At the time, it was purely part of putting the intention out there.

I wasn't expecting an instant result, and I wasn't sure that I would meet 'the one' this way. I was to get a very pleasant surprise! On the first day of my membership, I got an ice-breaker email from a guy on the site. We exchanged emails and he seemed great.

When we met I instantly liked him but I found myself holding back and not wanting to rush into anything. On our third date something strange happened. We were having a drink and this voice behind me, clear as day, said 'You really like him, more than you think'.

I turned round to see who had said it and as you can probably guess, there was no one there! It was my inner guidance speaking to me.

Within a few months we were talking about getting engaged. Next August I'm getting married! I've never been happier. Thank you Universe!

---

I hope the stories I've included in this chapter will inspire your to give the Law of Attraction a go. I'm passionate about Prosperity Wheels but this might not be the right tool for you. Experiment and see what works best for you. However you choose to communicate with the Universe I'm sure you will be delighted with your results.

# 9. Gratitude

Gratitude is a powerful energy that can transform your life. It requires you to make conscious choices and focus on those things that are good, right, or wonderful in your life.

Historically, the experience of gratitude has also been a focus of several world religions

## 9.1 The Importance of Gratitude

What is gratitude? Answer: it's a state of mind based on and ignited by beliefs. What is ungratefulness? It too is a state of mind based on and ignited by beliefs. In other words, we choose whether to be grateful for what we have or not. If you're not grateful you will probably travel through life always feeling disappointed.

The tangible and measurable evidence of the power of gratitude is the physical, financial, relational, emotional and spiritual things you manifest. Remember, thoughts become things - whether positive or negative.

So, focus on all the things you're grateful for rather than what's wrong in your life or what you don't have. When you're filled with gratitude you remove the fear and become an open channel for prosperity energy.

The more grateful you are the more abundance you will manifest as like attracts like. I don't want to sound like I'm preaching, but consciously utilising the power of gratitude is an important skill to master. Use gratitude to consciously and consistently attract the abundance and happiness that you desire.

"Never underestimate the power of a grateful heart when it comes to manifesting abundance" - Unknown

No matter how little you currently have always remember to be grateful; even if it's just gratitude for the lessons you're learning from your situation. If you don't like what you're manifesting, change your cosmic order to the Universe.

"God gave you a gift of 86,400 seconds today. Have you used one to say thank you?" - William A. Ward (Author of author of Fountains of Faith).

A question for you: "What are you truly and deeply grateful for right now?" You might like to spend a few minutes thinking about this.

Many prosperity teachers say we should create a gratitude list that we can review and add to each day. Your gratitude list should start with at least 10 things that you're grateful to.

Alternatively, spend a few minutes at the end of each day saying or thinking about the things you are grateful for. This might include good health or your ability to read and write. It could be gratitude for a safe home to live in and clean running water. You may feel grateful for your life with your soul mate, or your fantastic children that you're proud of.

These are just a few suggestions to get you started. You can be grateful for absolutely anything.

I was desperately sad when my mum passed away. However, I was still grateful that she had been a huge part of my life for 47 years. That thought carried me through some very dark days.

Whenever you see a sign that your abundance is increasing, even a very small sign, acknowledge it.  Be grateful for all your material possessions, your health, your body, your life, the people in your life; even the air you breathe.

In fact be grateful for everything you have. Trust me; you can never be too grateful!

"When you are grateful, fear disappears and abundance appears" - Anthony Robbins (American self-help author and motivational speaker).

If you don't want to create your own words of gratitude you might like to recite Brian Hinkle's Gratitude Prayer instead:

I thank you God/Goddess
I thank you Jesus
I thank the Higher Power
I thank the Ascended Masters
I thank you Saint Francis
I thank you Saint Germaine
I thank all those who guide me through my lives
And I send my loving gratitude
To each and every living creature
Amen

In case you're still struggling with the idea of gratitude here are some reasons to be grateful:

'I'm alive!'
'I'm still sane, what a miracle!'
'I have friends and people who care about me'
'I have a great family'
'I can afford to go out for dinner and have some fun'
'I have the time, funds and ability to pursue my choice of leisure activities'
'I can see, hear and walk'
'My health is good'
'I have free choice and free speech'
'I have a safe place to live and sleep'
'I have a job'
'I have a job/career that I love'
'I can consciously change my life if I really want to'
'I have a dream and I am moving towards it'

Finally, grateful people are happier, less depressed, less stressed and more satisfied with their lives and relationships. They also have higher levels of well-being. By expressing gratitude you will find more positive ways of coping with difficulties when they occur.

"Gratitude is the open door to abundance" - Unknown

## 9.2 Old Sioux Story

I came across this story a long time ago and it never fails to inspire me. For that reason I've included it in this book. I hope it touches you too.

The creator gathered all of creation and said "I want to hide something from the humans until they are ready for it. It is the realisation that they create their own reality". Where should I hide it?

The eagle said "Give it to me. I will take it to the moon"
The creator said "No, as one day they will go there and find it"
The salmon said "I will hide it in the bottom of the ocean"
"No, they will go there too" said the creator
The buffalo said "I will bury it in the great plains"
The creator said "they will cut into the skin of the earth and find it even there"
The grandmother mole, who lives in the breast of Mother Earth, and who has no physical eyes but sees with spiritual eyes, said "Put it inside them (the humans)"
And the creator said "It is done"

The moral of this story is – until we look inside ourselves and understand that we create our own destiny through our thoughts, we won't ever create the life we desire.

By: Author Unknown, Source Unknown

# 10. Frequently Asked Questions

I've tried to include all the most frequently asked questions in this section. I hope I've answered your questions too.

**Question:** Can you manifest anything and everything with a Prosperity Wheel?
**Answer:** Yes you can as long as it's realistic and you believe you can achieve it. Clearly not everyone can win the Lottery though.

**Question:** Why do I need to put a picture of myself in the middle of the wheel?
**Answer:** The Universe wants to know who to deliver all these good things to. Your photograph and the line that links it to each picture helps strengthen the intent.

**Question:** Should I remove items from my Prosperity Wheel as soon as I receive what I ordered?
**Answer:** It's up to you. Some people like to replace their pictures as soon as they've manifested what they want. Others like to leave the picture up there as a reminder of the power of intent.

**Question:** I'm more interested in doing a Prosperity Wheel than my wife is. Should I do a wheel for the family and one for myself, or just one for myself?
**Answer:** Focus on what's important to you. Unless your wife is 100% with you in prosperity work, don't put a joint picture on your wheel. If you do, then her energy will pull against yours and the wheel almost certainly won't work.

**Question:** Should I hang my Prosperity Wheel on a wall where I can see it, or should I keep it hidden away where no-one can see it?
**Answer:** Most prosperity teachers believe that we should place the wheel where it can be seen regularly. Some even claim the greatest successes come to those who make their wheel visible to others as well as themselves. Some prosperity teachers, like Catherine Ponder, say what is sacred is secret and so your Prosperity Wheel should be hidden away. I recommend you hang your Prosperity Wheel in a prominent place where you'll see it regularly (preferably daily).

**Question:** As my children are taking their school and university exams can I put some pictures on my wheel to increase their chance of exam success?
**Answer:** No, as your Prosperity Wheel is about you. Why not encourage your children to create their own Prosperity Wheel.

**Question:** Is it true that certain things should go on a particular coloured background?
**Answer:** Catherine Ponder and other prosperity teachers do suggest certain background colours according to your goals/aspirations. Personally I wouldn't get hung up on this: If a colour feels right to you then go for it. I always opt for gold card as gold is an excellent all-round prosperity colour.

**Question:** Do all of the images you use have to be colour photos?
**Answer:** The Universe responds to colour much better than black and white. I recommend that you use big, bright and colourful pictures, drawings and images. It's fine to include the odd black and white picture.

**Question:** Do I have to use magazine pictures? Can I print things off the internet and cut them out?
**Answer:** Absolutely. You can use any images that speak to you!

**Question:** If I decide not to use poster board is it OK to use a cork board instead?
**Answer:** I don't think there's a wrong way to do a Prosperity Wheel. Most people choose bright coloured card as it helps the Universe, but if it feels right to you, then go for it!

**Question:** I want a healthy/loving relationship, but I am having difficulty focusing on who/what I want. Do you have any advice for me?
**Answer:** Focus on the characteristics that you're looking for rather than having a person in mind. The Universe will do the rest.

**Question:** What do you do if your spouse rejects Prosperity Wheels or the Law of Attraction?
**Answer:** There is little point hanging your Prosperity Wheel somewhere that is going to cause conflict with your spouse so I suggest you put it somewhere that is your space. You can hide your Prosperity Wheel away if necessary, and the Universe will still do it's

best for you, but it's nice to see and enjoy your Prosperity Wheel regularly. If it is hidden away don't forget to look at it regularly.

**Question:** How often should I change my Prosperity Wheel?
**Answer:** Trust your instinct to tell you how often you should create or change your Prosperity Wheel. When it's time to change my wheel or make a new one, I notice that I start to get tired of the images.

**Question:** Can I put images that I've drawn myself on my Prosperity Wheel?
**Answer:** Yes. I always choose pictures from magazines because I can't draw, but if you have an artistic flair then use it. Don't forget to make your drawings colourful.

**Question:** Do I have to write an affirmation for each picture?
**Answer:** You don't have to label things, but it does add intent to your message to the Universe. Sometimes the affirmation makes your order clearer to the Universe than just a picture.

**Question:** I'm more analytical than visual. Is it alright to create a shopping list instead of pictures?
**Answer:** Absolutely! The Universe will respond to your order as long as the intent is strong enough. Don't forget to include the Universal Disclaimer though.

# 11. Quotes from Famous People

Here is a selection of prosperity quotes that I found as part of my research. You will find some of these strategically placed in the pages of this book. Others only appear in this chapter.

If any of these quotes talk to you write them down and put them somewhere you can see them. They may help to keep you focused when doubt creeps in.

"Though I am grateful for the blessings of wealth, it hasn't changed who I am. My feet are still on the ground. I'm just wearing better shoes"
**Oprah Winfrey** (American talk show host, actress, producer, and philanthropist)

"The primary cause of unhappiness is never the situation but your thoughts about it."
**Eckhart Tolle** (German/Canadian author of The Power of Now and A New Earth).

"Whatever we are waiting for - peace of mind, contentment, grace, the inner awareness of simple abundance - it will surely come to us, but only when we are ready to receive it with an open and grateful heart"

"Our deepest wishes are whispers of our authentic selves. We must learn to respect them. We must learn to listen"

"Become aware that you already possess all the inner wisdom, strength, and creativity needed to make your dreams come true.... We can learn to be the catalysts for our own change. . . .you already possess all you need to be genuinely happy."
**Sarah Ban Breathnach** (author of Simple Abundance and the found of the Simple Abundance Charitable Fund)

"Life is a field of unlimited possibilities"
**Deepak Chopra** (Indian-born, American physician, author and one of the pre-eminent leaders of the mind-body-spirit movement)

"The only place opportunity cannot be found is in a closed-minded person"
**Bo Bennett** (American businessman, author, philanthropist and motivational speaker)

"It's a kind of spiritual snobbery that makes people think they can be happy without money"
**Albert Camus** (French author, journalist, and philosopher)

"To attract money, you must focus on wealth. It is impossible to bring more money into your life when you are noticing you do not have enough, because that means you are thinking thoughts that you do not have enough"

"Every good thought, every good word, every good emotion, and every act of kindness, is lifting the vibration of your being to new heights. As you begin to raise your vibration, a new life and a new world will reveal itself to you"
**Rhonda Byrne** (author of The Secret)

"Empty pockets never held anyone back. Only empty heads and empty hearts can do that"
**Dr Norman Vincent Peale** (author of The Power of Positive Thinking)

"If you create opportunities, luck will follow"

"'Throughout the many ups and downs, the successes and the failures in my life, there has been a consistent and all-embracing belief that a positive attitude produces results"
**Noel Edmonds** (English entrepreneur, TV broadcaster, former Radio DJ and author of Positively Happy: Cosmic Ways to Change Your Life and Noel Edmonds - Positively Tranquil audio CD)

"Only those who dare to fail greatly can ever achieve greatly"
**Robert F Kennedy** (American politician and civil rights activist)

"If you take one step towards your dreams, your dreams will take multiple steps towards you"
**Christine Kane** (American folk singer/songwriter, acoustic guitarist and keynote speaker on women's issues, creativity, and business)

"Imagine that the Universe is like a cosmic kitchen with an infinite menu, just waiting to take and fulfil you orders"
**Patricia J Crane Ph.D.** (author of Ordering from the Cosmic Kitchen: The Essential Guide to Powerful, Nourishing Affirmations)

"If you see yourself as prosperous, you will be. If you see yourself as continually hard up, that is exactly what you will be"
**Robert Collier** (American author of self-help books)

"We make a living by what we get, but we make a life by what we give"
**Sir Winston Churchill** (British politician and statesman known for his leadership of the UK during the Second World War)

"If you want to change who you are, begin by changing the size of your dream. Even if you are broke, it does not cost you anything to dream of being rich. Many poor people are poor because they have given up on dreaming"
**Robert Kiyosaki** (Author of Rich Dad, Poor Dad)

"We can have whatever it is we choose I don't care how big it is"
**John Assaraf** (The Secret featured teacher)

"As you think, so shall you become"
**Bruce Lee** (martial arts legend and actor)

"God gave you a gift of 86,400 seconds today. Have you used one to say thank you?"
**William A. Ward** (Author of author of Fountains of Faith)

"It is better to risk starving to death then surrender. If you give up on your dreams, what's left?"
**Jim Carrey** (Actor, comedian, and film producer)

"When you are grateful fear disappears and abundance appears"
**Anthony Robbins** (American self-help author and motivational speaker)

"Go confidently in the direction of your dreams. Live the life you have imagined"

**Henry David Thoreau** (American author, philosopher and leading transcendentalist)

"The positive thinker sees the invisible, feels the intangible, and achieves the impossible"
**Author unknown**

"Gratitude is the open door to abundance"
**Author Unknown**

"I grew up on, you have to work hard for money, you have to work hard for money. And so I replaced that with, Money comes easily and frequently. Now in the beginning it feels like a lie, right? There's was a part of your brain, that will say, 'Oh you liar, it's hard.' So, you have to know this little tennis match that will go on for a while"
**Loral Langemeier** (Author of Put More Cash in Your Pocket: Turn What You Know into Dough, The Millionaire Maker: Act, Think, and Make Money the Way the Wealthy Do, Yes! Energy: The Equation to Do Less, Make More, The Millionaire Maker's Guide to Creating a Cash Machine for Life and The Millionaire Maker's Guide to Wealth Cycle Investing: Build Your Assets Into a Lifetime of Financial Freedom)

"Whatever you may be going through, the darkness is only temporary—it's not your destiny"
**Lisa Nichols** (The Secret featured teacher and co-author of the Chicken Soup for the Soul Series)

"If you're happy, you're wealthy! Happiness doesn't need a bank account."
**Sister Mary Christelle Macaluso R.S.M., O.F.N., Ph.D**

"Money is neither my god nor my devil. It is a form of energy that tends to make us more of who we already are, whether it's greedy or loving."
**Dan Millman** author of The Way of the Peaceful Warrior: A Book That Changes Lives, The Life You Were Born to Live: Finding Your Life Purpose, The Laws of Spirit: Simple, Powerful Truths for Making Life Work

"Abundance is not something we acquire. It is something we tune into."

**Wayne Dyer** author of Manifest Your Destiny, Wisdom of the Ages, There's a Spiritual Solution to Every Problem, 10 Secrets for Success and Inner Peace, The Power of Intention, Inspiration, Change Your Thoughts—Change Your Life, Excuses Begone, and now Wishes Fulfilled

"Not what we have but what we enjoy constitutes our abundance."
**Epicurus,** ancient Greek philosopher

"We tend to forget that happiness doesn't come as a result of getting something we don't have, but rather of recognizing and appreciating what we do have."
**Frederick Keonig** German inventor

"If we had no winter, the spring would not be so pleasant: if we did not sometimes taste of adversity, prosperity would not be so welcome."
**Anne Bradstreet** first American woman writer American poet to have her works published

"When we give, we simply make room for more to come in. When we become deeply, authentically generous, it signals to our abundant universe that there is a conduit open to receive and distribute. We become part of the vital natural system."
**Lenedra J. Caroll**, author of The Architecture of All Abundance

"Prosperity is not just having things. It is the consciousness that attracts the things. Prosperity is a way of living and thinking, and not just having money or things. Poverty is a way of living and thinking, and not just a lack of money or things."
**Eric Butterworth** author of Discover the Power Within You and The Universe Is Calling

"There is enough for all. The earth is a generous mother; she will provide in plentiful abundance food for all her children if they will but cultivate her soil in justice and in peace."
**Bourke Coekran** noted political orator

I choose the path of trust. I understand that I have little control in the external world. But I do have control of my reactions to it all.
**Susan Jeffers** author of Feel the Fear and Do It Anyway, End the Struggle and Dance With Life and Embracing Uncertainty

"Money is like any other relationship; it comes where it's invited and appreciated. It rarely comes when it's chased."
**Morgana Rae** (named one of 2012's Top Women in E-commerce by WE Magazine and author of Financial Alchemy)

"Never underestimate the power of a grateful heart when it comes to manifesting abundance"
**Author Unknown**

# 12. Further Reading

As you've chosen to read my book I'm assuming you're interested in the subject of prosperity, cosmic ordering or Prosperity Wheels, specifically. I've included a small selection of books and websites that you may be interested in:

## 12.1 Suggested Reading

| Book Title | Author |
| --- | --- |
| The Answer: Your Guide to Achieving Financial Freedom and Living an Extraordinary Life | John Assaraf and Murray Smith |
| Having It All: Achieving Your Life's Goals and Dreams | John Assaraf |
| The Secret | Rhonda Byrne |
| Ordering from the Cosmic Kitchen | Patricia Crane |
| Goals: How to Get Everything you Want | Brian Tracy |
| The Success Principles | Jack Canfield |
| From Credit Crunch to Pure Prosperity | Maggy Whitehouse |
| Opening Your Mind to Prosperity | Catherine Ponder |
| Ask And It Is Given - Learning to Manifest Your Desires | Esther & Jerry Hicks |
| Creating Money: Attracting Abundance | Sanaya Roman |
| De-junk Your Mind | Dawna Walter |
| Do What You Love; the Money Will Follow | Marsha Sinetar |
| Embracing Uncertainty | Susan Jeffers |
| Findhorn Book of Daily Abundance | Karen Hood-Caddy |
| The Abundance Book | John Randolph Price |
| The Power of Now: A Guide to Spiritual Enlightenment | Eckhart Tolle |
| You Can Heal Your Life | Louise L Hay |
| You Were Born Rich | Bob Proctor |
| Law of Attraction | Michael Losier |
| The Law Of Attraction: How to Make It Work For You | Esther and Jerry Hicks |
| The Key to Living the Law of Attraction: The Secret to Creating the Life of Your Dreams | Jack Canfield and D. D. Watkins |

| | |
|---|---|
| The Soulmate Secrets: Manifest the Love of Your Life with the Law of Attraction | Arielle Ford |
| Law of Attraction, Plain and Simple: Create the Extraordinary Life That You Deserve | Sonia Ricotti |
| The Law of Attraction: How To Get What You Want | Robert Collier |
| The Cosmic Ordering Service | Barbel Mohr |
| Rich Dad Poor Dad | Robert T. Kiyosaki |

"Gratitude is the open door to abundance"
**Unknown**

## 12.2 Useful Websites

| **Name** | **Website** |
|---|---|
| Abraham | www.abraham-hicks.com |
| Behind the Secret | http://www.thesecret.tv/behind.html |
| Bradley Thompson | www.advancedcosmicordering.com |
| Byron Katie | www.thework.com |
| Jack Canfield | www.jackcanfield.com |
| Elyse Hope Killoran | www evolutionarywealth.org |
| Free inspirational books, videos, courses, and downloads | www.whitedovebooks.co.uk |
| Morgana Rae | www.morganarae.com |

"Go confidently in the direction of your dreams. Live the life you have imagined" **- Henry David Thoreau** (American author, philosopher and leading transcendentalist)